MW01167254

CREATURES OF THE WILD

BEAR

GENERAL EDITOR:
ANN MALLARD
DEPARTMENT OF BIOLOGY, CITY COLLEGE OF SAN FRANCISCO

PHOTOGRAPHY BY
LEONARD LEE RUE III AND LEN RUE, JR.

CHARTWELL
BOOKS, INC.

This edition first published in 1998 by
PRC Publishing Ltd.
Kiln House,
210 New Kings Road,
London SW6 4NZ

© 1998 Promotional Reprint Company Ltd.

CHARTWELL BOOKS INC.
A division of BOOK SALES, INC

114 Northfield Avenue

Edison, New Jersey 08837

This edition was produced by American Graphic Systems, Inc., in cooperation with the
Northwest Natural History Society (NWNHS)
Design © 1998 American Graphic Systems, Inc.
Designed and captioned by Bill Yenne

All photographs are © 1998 Leonard Lee Rue III and Len Rue, Jr.

We are grateful for the information provided for this book by the US Fish & Wildlife Service

Note on terminology: According to the United States Endangered Species Act, the term "endangered" means a species is considered in danger of extinction throughout all or a significant portion of its range, while "threatened" is a less dire category, meaning a species is considered likely to become endangered, but not in danger of extinction.

ISBN 0 78580 8299

Printed and bound in China

BEAR

GENERAL EDITOR:

ANN MALLARD

DEPARTMENT OF BIOLOGY, CITY COLLEGE OF SAN FRANCISCO

It has been said that no other animal has so excited the human imagination as the bear. References to bears are found in literature, folk songs, legends, mythology, fairy tales, and cartoons. Bears are seen as a symbol of power and steadfastness. The American Indians had tremendous respect for the bear, and their shamans, or medicine men, were believed to share their power with the bear. They dressed in bearskins to impersonate the bear spirit and gain its support in the hunt, or to make use of its healing powers.

Among the Yuki Indians of Northern California such a man first dreamed of the grizzly, and then went off into the mountains to study its habits and behavior, and then to finally become transformed into a bear — a painful initiation which included growing body hair and finally (perhaps in a trance) becoming spiritually instructed in the bear songs and secrets. The bear-doctor, or *Wasit-lam-simi*, would return to the village dressed in bearskins, where he was able to cure bear bites and also to avenge wrongs in the community. In fact, the bear-doctors often murdered within the village, meting out a violent but effective justice. Many different Native American cultures felt a strong kinship with the bear, but especially in Northern California, where the grizzly was so common, the local tribes had to incorporate this fearsome bear into their culture as a way to cope, both physically and psychologically. In more recent times there is ample evidence that the legends of Yeti, the Abominable Snowman of the Himalayas, and sasquatch, the big foot of North America, have been perpetuated by sightings of large bears walking on their hind legs — and may even have been originally based on sightings of bears.

Scientifically, bears are all members of the family *Ursidae*, which includes the giant pandas of China (subfamilies *Ailuroponinae*), the spectacled bears of South America (*Tremarctinae*) and *Ursinae*, which includes all other bears, including the sloth bears, Malayan sun bears and "true bears."

True bears include the three types of bears found in North America, as well as the Asiatic black bear (*Selenarctos thibetanus*). The smallest, and most common, American bear is the American black bear (*Ursus americanus*), which may weigh as little as 125 pounds for a young female to 400 pounds for a large male. The largest of our bears is the polar bear (*Ursus maritimus*). A big male can weigh in at as much as 1,200 pounds, and even the smaller females are 400 pounds. All the brown bears belong to one species (*Ursus arctos*), but are separated into two subspecies, the Alaskan Brown Bear, (*Ursus arctos middendorffi*), and the grizzly bear (*Ursus arctos horribilis*). Grizzlies are nearly as large as polar bears — a large male can reach 1,000 pounds — but females are considerably smaller (200 to 600 pounds).

Although the American black bear is found only in North America, it is by far the most numerous type of bear in the world. There are about 700,000 black bears in North America (with over half of these being in Canada). The polar bear is found throughout the arctic regions, including the northern edges of Asia and Europe, but most of these bears are in Canada (15,000 in Canada, while Russia and Norway each have about 5,000). The brown bear, which is a descendant or close relative of the legendary, but now extinct, European cave bear (*Ursus spelaeus*), is also found in both Europe and Asia. While there are about 70,000 brown

Opposite: A black bear licking insects from a spruce tree. Black bears are omnivores, although about 85 percent of their diet consists of vegetation.

Opposite: The black bear's teeth, which number 42, are primarily molars designed for grinding rather than tearing.

bears in North America, there are over 100,000 in Russia, and small populations are still found in Romania, and in northern Japan.

Alaska probably has the highest concentration of bears in North America, and it has large numbers of all three North American types. Black bears inhabit most of Alaska's forests, and polar bears frequent the pack ice and tundra of extreme northern and western Alaska. The brown bears are found from the islands of southeastern Alaska to the arctic. In Alaska there are an estimated 5,000 polar bears, over 35,000 grizzly or brown bears, and more than 50,000 black bears.

THE BLACK BEAR

The American black bear (*Ursus americanus*) inhabits wooded and mountainous areas throughout most of North America, from northern Alaska, east across Canada to Labrador and Newfoundland, and south through much of the United States, and into the central Mexican states of Nayarit and Tamaulipas.

Black bears are not necessarily "black" — their shaggy hair varies in color from white through yellowish, or cream-colored to reddish, chocolate brown, cinnamon brown, and black. However, most black bears are indeed black or a darker shade of brown. Although these bears are over five feet long and weigh over 250 pounds, they can run as fast as 25 miles per hour to chase their prey, and they are skillful tree climbers. While black bears are capable of standing and walking on their hind legs, the usual posture is on all fours. The black bear's characteristic shuffle results from walking flat-footed, with the hind legs slightly longer than the front legs. Each paw has five strong, nonretractable claws used for tearing, digging, climbing trees and hunting. One blow from a powerful front paw is enough to kill an adult deer, although black bears are generally content to scavenge carrion. In spite of their size and strength, black bears are surprisingly agile and careful in their movements.

Throughout the bears' range, their primary habitat is characterized by relatively inaccessible terrain and thick underbrush, especially where there is plenty of food in the form of shrubs.

Along the north Pacific coast, bears inhabit forests of redwood, sitka spruce, and hemlock, but also visit the meadows and high tidelands to forage. They are common in the pine and fir forests of the Sierra and have become infamous in California parks as they frequent campground areas searching for easy food. In the Southwest, prime black bear habitat is restricted to mountainous areas of chaparral or pinon pine and juniper woodland between 3,000 to 9,000 feet in altitude. Bears occasionally move out of the chaparral into more open sites and feed on prickly pear cacti.

The spruce and fir forests are home to black bears in the Rockies, but they also like wet meadows, avalanche-formed canyons and roadsides where people throw away food, as well as sidehills and ridgetops. Black bears in the southern Appalachian Mountains survive in forests of oak and hickory. In the coastal areas of the Southeast, black bears inhabit a mixture of woods and swampy areas. In the Northeast, they live in hardwood forests of beech, maple, birch and conifers. Thick, swampy areas provide excellent cover. Corn crops and hardwood leaves are also common sources of food in some sections of the Northeast.

One of the reasons this large animal is still common in North America is that it has adapted to living in areas frequented by man. However, unlike the Native Americans, the European settlers in America were not

Opposite: A young black bear climbing a tree. Note that the configuration of their claws, makes black bears are the best climbers among all North American bears. Brown and grizzly bears climb rarely if at all, but black bears do so easily and often.

COMPARATIVE BLACK BEAR POPULATION DATA

UNITED STATES TOTAL	**300,000**
States with highest concentrations:	
Alaska	100,000
Montana	30,000
Washington	30,000
Idaho	25,000
Oregon	25,000
California	15,000
Colorado	10,000
Michigan	7,500
Pennsylvania	7,500
CANADA TOTAL	**400,000**
Provinces with highest concentrations:	
British Columbia	100,000
Ontario	75,000
Quebec	60,000
Alberta	40,000
Manitoba	30,000
Saskatchewan	30,000
New Brunswick	15,000
Yukon	10,000

comfortable with a policy of "co-existence" with bears, and bear populations have been reduced considerably in the last 400 years. The black bear once lived throughout most of the 48 contiguous United States, but hunting and agriculture drove them into heavily forested areas, where today about 75,000 to 80,000 survive as small, separated populations in sparsely populated wooded regions and under protection in national parks. Today they are numerous and thriving in their protected habitats, and recovering from the tremendous reduction in their numbers that occurred in the days of early settlement.

During the eighteenth and early nineteenth centuries, black bears were hunted almost to extinction on the East Coast. Many states paid bounties for bears, and as late as 1977, there was still a bounty law on the books in Highland County, Virginia (although, at that time, it had been more than 30 years since the last bounty was paid). In addition to hunting — often encouraged by the bounties — black bear numbers were reduced

Opposite: The polar bear's coat is not actually white but transparent. The slight yellowish tinge seen here comes from blond underhairs and from oxidation that occurs after exposure to the sun during the long days of the Arctic summer.

COMPARATIVE AVERAGE SIZE DATA
(Inches, centimeters in parentheses)

BLACK BEAR

Height (at shoulders)	36(91)
Length	60(152)

POLAR BEAR

Height (at shoulders)	64(161)
Length	96(244)

BROWN BEAR

Height (at shoulders)	60(152)
Length	100(260)

in eastern North America by logging and burning, clearing land for crops and grazing, and all the encroachments associated with expanding settlement. By the early twentieth century, the once-common black bear was becoming rare in the East, and could be found only in remote, mountainous areas of Georgia, Kentucky, Maryland, North Carolina, Pennsylvania, Tennessee, Virginia, and West Virginia. However, they were still commonly seen in the Mountain and Western states and provinces of the United States and Canada. As small farms failed and people moved back to the cities, bear habitat slowly recovered and populations started to increase in the East. The early establishment of national parks and national forests in the East helped save the black bear in that region.

Today, a major threat to the American black bear is widespread poaching, or illegal killing, to supply Asian markets with bear gall bladders and paws, considered to have medicinal value in China, Japan, and Korea. The demand for these parts also affects grizzly and polar bears. The Convention on International Trade in Endangered Species of Wild

Fauna and Flora (CITES), a treaty among more than 120 nations, provides measures to curb illegal trade in wildlife and wildlife products across international boundaries, helping to protect the black bear from poaching. The US Fish & Wildlife Service is the agency responsible for the United States government's compliance with the CITES treaty.

Although attitudes concerning bears and other game animals have changed, and wildlife laws protecting black bears and other animals have been enacted, the understanding of the black bear, its behavior, and its habitat requirements remained incomplete until the 1960s.
More has been learned about the habits and needs of the black bear in the last quarter of the twentieth century than in all of recorded history because we now have methods and techniques for safely trapping, immobilizing, and handling these powerful animals. Thanks to this new knowledge and understanding, and better management, black bear populations have

Opposite: A big polar bear fords a shallow stream. Powerful swimmers, these big mammals can cross any water obstacle with ease.

COMPARATIVE MAXIMUM WEIGHT DATA
(Pounds, kilograms in parentheses)

BLACK BEAR
Contiguous United States	800(360)
Alaska	500(225)
Canada	800(360)

POLAR BEAR
Alaska	1,500(675)
Canada	1,700(765)

BROWN BEAR
Contiguous United States	1,200(540)
Alaska	1,600(720)
Canada	1,000(450)

recovered significantly, although they are not out of danger. The survival of black bear populations must also be attributed to this bear's keen intelligence and adaptability, which have made it possible for this bear to learn new techniques of survival in a world dominated by humans.

Black bears are opportunistic feeders, making use of many available food sources. While they prefer berries, nuts, grass, and other plants, they also eat carrion, small animals, and fish. Spring, after the bears' emergence from winter dens, is a period of relative food scarcity. Bears tend to lose weight during this period, and continue to subsist partly off body fat stored during the preceding fall. They take advantage of any succulent and protein-rich foods that are available at this time of year. However, these are not typically available in sufficient quantity to maintain body weight. As summer approaches, a variety of berry crops become available. Summer is generally a period of abundant and diverse foods for black bears, enabling them to recover from the energy deficits of winter and spring.

Black bears are not active predators. They never feed on animals larger than themselves, unless there is an opportunity to take over a kill made by another predator. Only a small portion of the diet of bears consists of meat, and this is mainly insects, such as ants, termites and beetles. As a result, the diet of black bears is high in carbohydrates and low in proteins and fats. Consequently, they generally prefer foods with high protein or fat content, and thus their propensity for "people food," such as they are able to scavenge from garbage cans, especially at campgrounds. Since the 1970s, however, campground management has discouraged this through the use of bear-proof garbage cans.

Opposite: A mother polar bear and her cubs. While other bears will often be born into litters of three, twins are most common among polar bears and only one time in 10 will there be a third cub.

COMPARATIVE LONGEVITY DATA

BLACK BEAR

Maximum, Natural Environment	31
Maximum, Captive Environment (Zoo)	44
Average	18

POLAR BEAR

Maximum, Natural Environment	34
Maximum, Captive Environment (Zoo)	41
Average	25

BROWN BEAR

Maximum, Natural Environment	30
Maximum, Captive Environment (Zoo)	44
Average	25

Generally black bears are out and foraging for food at dawn and at dusk, although "campground bears" or "peanut butter bears" have adapted to people by learning to forage in campsites late at night. During periods of inactivity, black bears utilize bed sites in forest habitat; these sites generally consist of a simple, shallow depression in the forest leaf litter. When fall approaches, black bears must eat large amounts of food in order to gain enough weight to sustain them through the winter when there is almost no food available.

As the weather turns cold, they search out a den in a cave, under a log, or even up in a tree. In populated areas bears may den in culverts or under buildings. Technically, bears do not truly hibernate, because their physiology doesn't actually change; their heart rate doesn't slow down appreciably, nor does their body temperature decrease. In winter, most bears certainly sleep for long periods and survive on their reserves of body fat, but during periods of relatively warm weather, they may awaken and take short excursions outside. Also, it is during this period of "hibernation" that female bears give birth and nurse their cubs through the first, most vulnerable, weeks.

Females reach maturity at four to five years of age, and males about a year later. Black bears breed every second or third spring, and the mating season generally peaks between June and mid-July. Courting and mating is the one period of real interaction for adult bears, which are otherwise very solitary animals. Pregnancy does not begin immediately after mating, however. As in many mammals, females are able to delay the implantation of the fertilized egg in the uterus until the fall, so that they are pregnant mainly during the winter and the cubs will be born in early spring, while they are still in their dens. Pregnancy generally lasts about seven months. However, if food was scarce and the mother has not gained enough fat to sustain herself during hibernation, as well as provide for her developing cubs, the embryos do not develop. Births occur mainly in January and February, and the young cubs are naked and blind, weighing only a half a pound each. A mother may give birth to a single cub or a litter, but twins are most common. By spring thaw, when the bears start leaving their dens, the cubs are fur-balls of energy, inquisitive and playful. They are weaned between July and September of their first year, but stay with their mother through the first full winter. They are usually independent by their second winter. Cubs mature slowly, and their survival is totally dependent on the skill of the mother in teaching her cubs what to eat, where and how to find food, where to den, and when and where to seek shelter from bad weather or other danger.

The mother and her cubs develop highly evolved behavioral relationships, probably as a result of the slow maturation of the cubs and the tremendous amount of learning that must be passed on during their family

Opposite: The grizzly bear, as seen here, has no natural predators, and no other animal will attempt to fight with an adult grizzly one-on-one.

period. Even as adults, black bears possess a high level of intelligence, which shows itself in their curiosity, exploratory behavior, and in their excellent memory. Black bears have been known to open door latches and to unscrew jar lids. They even recognize vehicles and uniforms.
Marking is an important method of communicating for these solitary animals. Black bears leave their scent by rubbing trees with their heads and shoulders, or with their rumps. They may claw or bite a tree, or even push it over.

In general bears have home ranges but do not generally establish strict territories that they will defend against other bears. However, adult females with cubs may establish territories during the summer.
Spacing of individual bears at other times of the year is likely maintained through a dominance hierarchy system. Because bears are generally solitary, except for breeding and raising young, males and females have separate home ranges. The size of a home range is determined by food abundance and availability, and can be as small as a square mile or as great as 100 square miles. Rugged terrain and dense shrubs provide cover, and trees

are also used to escape from danger. When possible, black bears will choose streams surrounded by dense shrubbery as travel corridors to and from food sources. Daily movements are influenced greatly by temperature and food availability. During the heat of the day, they will seek shade in dense underbrush. Black bears also try to avoid humans and are considered nonaggressive except when injured, protecting their young, or protecting themselves.

In the wild, black bears live to be about 18, although in captivity one bear is known to have survived to the age of 44. As bears get older, they lose their teeth, and may starve to death, or they may be weakened by parasites, such as worms. Younger bears are often killed by various accidents, including, of course, being shot by hunters or struck by cars or trains. An indirect, but critically important, cause of mortality is habitat loss.

Although the American black bear is fairly abundant through out most of its range in the United States and Canada, the populations of two subspecies found in the southeastern United States, the Louisiana black bear and the Florida black bear, still face decline, mainly due to habitat loss and degradation. In 1992, the US Fish & Wildlife Service listed the Louisiana black bear (*Ursus americanus luteolu*) as a threatened species under the Endangered Species Act, meaning it "could become in danger of extinction throughout all or a significant portion of its range in the foreseeable future."

The Louisiana black bear is one of 16 recognized subspecies of the American black bear. It often winters in hollow cypress trees, either in or along swamps, lakes, or riverbanks in the bottom-land of the Tensas and Atchafalaya river basins. These bears are mobile and live on a variety of foods, particularly leaves. They travel long distances and are often seen throughout the lower Mississippi River area, although it is unknown whether breeding numbers exist outside Louisiana. The Louisiana black bears are featured as a priority species for protection and management on the Tensas and Atchafalaya River National Wildlife Refuges, state-owned

Opposite: A grizzly in Alaska, where bears of the species *Ursus arctos* are largest, possibly as heavy as a ton.

lands, and on certain important privately-owned tracts, such as Deltic Farms near Tallulah, Louisiana. In fact, the American black bear is protected in the states of Louisiana, Mississippi, and Texas, due to its close resemblance to the threatened Louisiana sub-species. The Florida black bear is also a candidate for protection under the Endangered Species Act. The US Fish & Wildlife Service monitors the animals' status and takes appropriate measures to ensure its conservation.

THE POLAR BEAR

The polar bear (*Ursus maritimus*) is the largest member of the bear family, with the exception of Alaskan brown bears, which equal polar bears in size. Male polar bears are about five feet tall at the shoulder and generally weigh about 1,000 pounds, although they may reach 1,500 pounds. Females usually weigh about 500 pounds, but may reach 700 pounds. Part of the reason for the polar bear's weight is that it stores a four-inch-thick layer of fat to keep it warm. To support this layer of fat, it is estimated that the polar bear must consume an entire seal every week.

Opposite: A grizzly cub, as seen here, may reach 80 pounds by the age of six months.

Although the polar bear's coat appears white, each individual hair is actually a transparent, hollow tube which tunnels the heat of the sun's rays to the bear's darker skin and helps it stay warm. Light reflected from the coat makes the polar bear appear white. During the summer months, adult bears molt, or gradually shed their coats, and grow new ones, which look pure white. By the following spring, the sun has caused their coats to turn a yellowish shade, and more color may be added by stains from seal oils. The polar bear's coat also helps it blend in with its snow-covered environment, a useful hunting adaptation.

The polar bear's front legs have the appearance of being slightly bow-legged and pigeon-toed, and they have fur which covers the bottoms of its paws. These adaptations help the polar bear by keeping it from slipping on the ice. Its head and nose are longer and narrower than other bears' and it is known to have an extremely keen sense of smell, enabling it to detect a seal several miles away. Its ears are smaller and furred inside for protection.

Known as *Nanuuq* (pronounced na-NOOK) by the native Inuit

COMPARATIVE POLAR BEAR POPULATION DATA
(Estimated)

UNITED STATES TOTAL	2,000
States with highest concentrations:	
Alaska	2,000
CANADA TOTAL	15,000
Provinces with highest concentrations:	
Northwest Territories	12,000
Manitoba	1,500

(formerly known as Eskimo) people, the polar bear lives only in the far north of the Northern Hemisphere, specifically on the Arctic ice cap, and spends most of its time in coastal areas.

Polar bears are found on the northern and northwestern coasts of Alaska in the United States, and they are also widely dispersed in Canada, extending from the northern Arctic islands south to the Hudson Bay area. They are also found in Greenland, on islands off the coast of Norway and on the northern coast of Russia, mostly in Siberia. There are estimated to be 28,000 polar bears worldwide, with over half in Canada, and most of the remainder equally divided between Norway, Russia and Alaska.

Polar bears tend to lead very nomadic lifestyles and generally do not travel in groups. They may roam the tundra, but never venture very far inland, preferring to keep close to the ocean and their food sources. Quite often, polar bears are found drifting on ice floes in northern waters. A few have been observed near the North Pole, but the heavy, year-round ice there provides poor seal hunting, so most are found further south, where the ice is thinner and broken.

Some polar bears may make extensive north-south migrations as the pack ice recedes northward in the spring and advances southward in the fall. They also may travel long distances during the breeding season to find mates, or in search of food. It was once believed that polar bears migrated throughout the Arctic, but modern research suggests that there are actually a number of distinct groups. Russian and American scientists are investigating the possibility that the polar bears in the Bering Sea area are of a single group that winters from Wrangel Island south along the Asian coast, and in the central Bering Sea as far as Saint Matthew Island. These bears seldom have contact with those found in the Beaufort Sea east of Point Barrow, Alaska.

Polar bears can run quite swiftly, but are most agile when they are swimming in the sea. They are excellent swimmers, and can reach speeds of up to six miles per hour in the water. They are good divers, too. When being pursued by hunters in open water, polar bears have been known to escape by plunging 10 to 15 feet below the surface and resurfacing a good distance away. They have also been seen swimming up to 100 miles away from ice or land.

Because the polar bear rarely eats vegetation, it is considered a carnivore, or meat-eater. In the summer months, however, the bears eat berries and various other vegetation. The ringed seal is the polar bear's primary prey. Seals have adapted to life in the Arctic Ocean, but they must surface to breathe and go ashore to reproduce, and so polar bears evolved to prey upon this rich food source. A polar bear may stalk a seal by waiting quietly for it to emerge from its blow hole, or "atluk," an opening seals make in the ice allowing them to breathe or climb out of the water to rest.

The polar bear will often have to wait for hours for a seal to emerge. Because the polar bear's coat is camouflaged against the whiteness of the ice and snow, the seal may not see the stalking bear. Polar bears eat only

Opposite: An adult grizzly exhibiting the aggressiveness that make them a dangerously unpredictable animal.

the seal's skin and blubber, or fat, and the remaining meat is an important food source for other animals of the Arctic. For example, Arctic foxes feed almost entirely on the remains of polar bear kills during the winter. The carcasses of whales, seals, and walruses are also important food sources for polar bears. In fact, because of their acute sense of smell, polar bears can sense carcasses from many miles away.

Polar bears also prey on walruses, but, because of the walruses' ferocity and size, bears are usually successful at preying only on their young. Encounters between an adult walrus and a polar bear are violent and bloody, and can end in defeat for either party. In fact the walrus is the only animal that the polar bear really fears.

Polar bears reach breeding maturity at three to five years of age, and males may travel great distances in search of female mates. While breeding usually takes place in April, like other bears, the female can delay the implantation of the fertilized egg so that the embryos develop during the fall and are born in the den in winter. Like other bears, the pregnancy will be continued only if the mother has had a stable enough supply of food to sustain herself, as well as the developing cubs, through the winter.

Unlike other bears, male polar bears do not hibernate, and in October and November, male polar bears begin to head out on the pack ice, where they spend the winter. Pregnant females seek sites on the mainland or on sea ice to dig large dens in snow where they will give birth and spend the winter. The temperature inside the polar bear's den can be up to 40 degrees warmer than outside. Usually two cubs are born in December or January. When the cubs first arrive, they are blind, hairless, and no bigger than squirrels. However, the cubs grow rapidly from the rich milk, high in butterfat, that is provided by their mother.

When spring comes, the mother bear leads her cubs to the coast near the open sea, where seals and walruses are plentiful. The cubs remain with their mother for 30 months, and they continue to nurse for 18 to 24 months, longer than any other bear cubs. Because of this, most adult female polar bears breed only every third year. While she is raising them, the mother will fiercely protect her cubs from perceived danger.

Polar bears have traditionally played an important role in the culture and livelihood of Inuit people, and indeed, the spiritual guardians of Inuit shamans were usually polar bears. They believed that the spirits of people and bears sometimes inhabited each others' bodies. Inuits and other native

Opposite: A grizzly makes its way across a steep sidehill. Grizzlies will often remain in the open, and are easy to spot at a comfortable distance.

COMPARATIVE BROWN BEAR POPULATION DATA
(Estimated)

UNITED STATES TOTAL	45,000
States with highest concentrations:	
Alaska	43,500
Montana	1,000
CANADA TOTAL	25,000
Provinces with highest concentrations:	
British Columbia	13,000
Yukon	6,000
Northwest Territories	5,000

people of the North have traditionally depended on these mammals for food and clothing. As such, they are exempted from the Marine Mammal Protection Act of 1972, which protects the species in the United States. This law prohibits hunting of polar bears by non-natives and established special conditions for the importation of polar bears or their parts and products into the United States. Inuit people and other Alaska natives are allowed to hunt some polar bears for subsistence and handicraft purposes. The Soviet Union had instituted a similar hunting ban in 1956.

An international conservation agreement for polar bears signed in 1976 by the United States, the Soviet Union, Norway, Canada, and Denmark (on behalf of Greenland) also provides for cooperative management of polar bears. For its part, the former Soviet Union had set aside Wrangel Island as a wildlife preserve. The most important refuge in the United States is in Alaska's Arctic National Wildlife Refuge.

The US Fish & Wildlife Service and the National Biological Service work together to monitor and study polar bears in Alaska, where they number about 5,000. Cooperative efforts with Canada involve monitoring polar bears in the Beaufort Sea, and the agencies work with the Russian government to monitor the animals in the Chukchi Sea. The US Fish & Wildlife Service also undertakes education and outreach efforts to inform the public about how polar bears can be protected from over-harvest.

In Alaska, demands for oil, natural gas, and other resources have led to some conflicts between polar bears and humans, so the US Fish &

Wildlife Service provides expertise to industries on how to minimize conflicts with bears while conducting their operations. A number of protective measures have been taken to reduce human activities along the coasts while polar bears are in their dens. This is a time of year when the animals are most sensitive to outside disturbances.

BROWN BEARS

A symbol of America's wilderness, the grizzly, or brown, bear (*Ursus arctos*) is one of the largest North American land mammals. There are two subspecies of *Ursus arctos* in North America, and they were once thought to be two distinct species. These are the

Above: A black bear on an open hillside. Because they are North America's most numerous bear species, black bears inhabit more of their former range than brown bears, and a wide variety of habitat types.

Above: A black bear in the northeastern United States, where the species is almost invariably black. In other parts of the continent, over a quarter of the population may be various shades of brown.

Alaskan brown bear (*Ursus arctos middendorffi*) of Alaska and the grizzly bear (*Ursus arctos horribilis*), found elsewhere. A third subspecies, the California golden bear, became extinct early in the twentieth century. The historic range of *Ursus arctos* once covered much of North America, from the mid-plains westward to California, and from central Mexico north throughout Alaska and Canada. *Ursus arctos* also ranged in extremely small numbers from western Europe — as far south as Italy — and the Middle East, to eastern Siberia and the Himalayan region, Hokkaido in Japan, and in the Atlas Mountains of northwest Africa.

Unlike the black bear, the brown and grizzly bears have a rather concave face, high-humped shoulders, and long, curved claws. They also have shorter, rounder ears than the black bear. The brown bear's thick fur varies from light brown or cinnamon to nearly black, and sometimes looks frosty-looking, hence the name "grizzly," or "silvertip."

Above: A pair of three-month-old black bear cubs. At this age, bear cubs typically are not fully weaned.

Above: This eight-week-old black bear cub has grown to a weight of five pounds from a birth weight of about 13 ounces. Helpless at birth, the cub has been walking for three weeks.

Today, the grizzly bear is found throughout Alaska, British Columbia, the Yukon, the Northwest Territories, and Alberta. However, the grizzly still inhabits only about two percent of its original range in the lower 48 United States. Between 1800 and 1975, grizzly bear populations in the lower 48 United States are thought to have decreased from estimates of more than 50,000 to roughly 1,000. Estimates on the continent as a whole indicate a current population of about 66,000. The grizzly was eliminated from the Great Plains and much of the West by the late nineteenth century as mountainous areas were settled.

California was prime grizzly habitat, and the California golden bear roamed in the thousands over the grasslands and coast ranges. Early explorers in California reported it was not unusual to see 50 or 60 of these great bears in a day. As the Spanish settlers began raising cattle in these valleys, the bears discovered a new food source, and it is said that

Above: Though this 18-month-old black bear has been weaned for more than a year, he still may travel with, and be socially dependent on, his mother.

Opposite: Bears are rare among four-legged mammals in their ability to stand on two legs with ease.

populations increased accordingly. But not for long. The repeating rifle sealed the fate of the grizzly in California, as in most of the rest of the lower 48. Professional grizzly hunters set out to clear the land of these dangerous beasts, and often bragged of shooting five to six of the huge animals in a single day. The most famous grizzly hunters kept tallies and claimed the lives of 200 or more bears during their hunting days. The California grizzly is still designated as the state mammal of California, and holds a central position on the state flag. However the Golden Bear was last seen in the Sierra Nevada in 1929, and has long been considered to be extinct.

In 1975, the US Fish & Wildlife Service listed the grizzly bear as a threatened species under the Endangered Species Act, meaning it was considered likely to become in danger of extinction within all or a significant portion of its range. Many of the current threats to the survival of

Above: A young black bear explores a rotting tree stump for colonies of ants or termites, which make a delicious lunch for a bear.

Opposite: A black bear yearling scampers up a tree exhibiting their natural proclivity for climbing.

grizzly bears are associated with degradation of habitat, because they require such a large range, and unlike the black bear, grizzlies have not adapted to life in close proximity to man. Some grizzlies are accidentally killed by hunters who mistake them for black bears, which are legal game, but largely, grizzly hunting is a thing of the past in the lower 48 states.

Today, in this area, grizzlies can be found in Wyoming, Montana, Idaho, and Washington. The highest concentration is in the northwestern Montana Rockies, in and around Glacier National Park, where there are at least 350 grizzlies living, and there are approximately 250 grizzlies in or around Yellowstone National Park. However, other populations in the lower United States are dangerously low: about 25 individuals in the Selkirk Mountains (northern Idaho and northeast Washington), another 20 in the Cabinet-Yaak ecosystem (northern Idaho and western Montana), and up to 20 in the North Cascades.

Above: A large adult black bear ambles through a deep hardwood forest where they can navigate with ease.

Above: A black bears in a Pennsylvania forest. Bears are larger and heavier in the north than in the south. They typically average about 400 pounds in Southern states, while 800-pound black bears have been recorded in Pennsylvania and Manitoba.

In Alaska, brown bears and grizzlies are estimated to number more than 40,000. The highest densities and largest populations live along the coast. These are usually the subspecies, known as the Alaskan brown or Kodiak bear (*Ursus arctos middendorffi*). Kodiak brown bears are the largest land carnivores in the world. A male is easily twice as large as the inland grizzly in Alaska. There are about 25,000 grizzly bears in Canada, including 15,000 in British Columbia alone. In Eurasia there are an estimated 100,000 brown bears, with about 70,000 of those living in Siberia. Larger than the black bear, male brown or grizzly bears stand on their hind legs at about seven feet tall. There is a tremendous range of size, however. Male grizzlies weigh from 350 to 850 pounds, and occasionally more than 1,000, with the heavier bears being found in the northern areas. Females are smaller, usually weighing between 200 and 400 pounds. The species is largest along the coast of southern Alaska and

Above: A mother polar bear and her cubs.

Above: As seen here, polar bear cubs weigh more than 100 pounds at six months, but they will not be fully grown for eight or nine years. At this time, they may weigh more than 1,000 pounds.

on nearby islands, where the Alaskan brown bear or Kodiak bear can weigh as much as 2,000 pounds.

Brown bears move with a slow, lumbering walk, although they are capable of moving very quickly and can easily catch a black bear. They are mainly terrestrial, although they can often be found swimming or preying upon fish in the water. Adults are generally thought to be unable to climb trees, although some experienced observers will take exception to this notion.

Ursus arctos has an excellent sense of smell, and is said to be able to follow the scent of a rotting carcass for more than two miles. These bears have human-level hearing, but relatively poor eyesight. They are extremely strong and have good endurance. They can kill a cow with one blow, outrun a horse, outswim any land mammal, including humans, and drag a dead elk uphill.

Above: As with most bear species, polar bear cubs usually remain close to their mother as she teaches them to hunt and to protect themselves.

Above: The mother polar bear carefully monitors her young. The cubs will continue to nurse for two years and will remain socially dependent upon her into their third year.

Ursus arctos needs a very large home range. This is calculated as being 50 to 300 square miles for females, and 200 to 500 square miles for males. Home ranges overlap extensively, and there is no evidence of territorial defense, although bears are generally solitary. Occasionally, bears may gather in large numbers at major food sources and form family foraging groups.

Seasonal movements from range to range have been observed, with individuals sometimes traveling hundreds of miles during the autumn to reach areas of favorable food supplies, such as salmon streams and areas of high berry production — wilderness areas of diverse forests interspersed with moist meadows and grasslands in or near mountains. In the spring, these bears usually range at lower elevations, and go into higher altitudes for their winter hibernation. Farther north these bears also occupy a

Above: A young polar bear taking a nap. Except for pregnant females, polar bears do not hibernate.

Above: A polar bear awakens from sleeping in the snow. Far from making the bear cold while it is asleep, the snow provides insulation to help on retention of body heat.

variety of habitats, but prefer open areas, such as tundra, alpine meadows and coastlines. Grizzlies were common on the Great Plains prior to the arrival of European settlers. In Siberia, the species occurs primarily in forests, while European bears are restricted mainly to mountain woodlands.

Although a standing bear is commonly perceived to be in a threatening pose, bears stand when they are simply curious or surveying their surroundings. Otherwise they generally remain on all fours. Adult brown bears have little to fear from other wild animals, but their cubs may fall prey to mountain lions, wolves, and other bears if they stray too far from their mothers. The only social bonds formed are be-tween females and young. During the breeding season, males may fight over females and guard their mates for several weeks. The highest-ranking individuals are large adult males, although the

Above: A polar bear nibbling on a weed. Though they are the most carnivorous of North American bears, polar bears will also eat such vegetable matter as berries or kelp if it is available.

Above: A polar bear in her "day bed." All bears prepare several of these throughout their range, and these are used repeatedly. They differ from dens in that they are on the surface of the ground and they are not used for hibernating.

most aggressive bears are females with young, and the least aggressive and lowest-ranking are adolescents.

    Except for mating and caring for the young, brown bears primarily
lead solitary lives, spending most of their time foraging, or looking for
food. *Ursus arctos* is North America's largest omnivore, meaning it eats
both plants and other animals. However, about 80 to 90 percent of the
animals' food is green vegetation, wild fruits and berries, as well as nuts,
and bulbs or roots of certain plants. These bears also like insects, and
sometimes tear rotten logs apart and turn over heavy rocks in search of
insects or their larvae. They also dig mice, ground squirrels and marmots
out of their burrows. In the Canadian Rockies, grizzly bears are quite carnivorous, hunting moose, elk, mountain sheep and goats, and occasionally
black bears are preyed upon.

    When the open pit garbage dumps in Yellowstone National Park,
which had been a source of grizzly food for 80 years, were closed in the

Above and opposite: A pair of young
polar bears at play. Cubs will wrestle
with one another almost before they
can stand, and this "play fighting" will
continue until the bears are several
years old.

1970s, grizzlies were observed to readily adapt to feeding on an abundant population of elk calves. In Alaska, the species has been observed to eat carrion, and occasionally capture young calves of caribou and moose. For brown bears along the west coast of Canada and in Alaska, salmon is an important food source.

Brown bears must eat enough to store huge amounts of fat needed to sustain them through their long winter sleep. The ability of these bears to eat large quantities of rich food and store fat without suffering from heart disease or cholesterol problems is of great interest to medical scientists, who hope that if they can understand how grizzlies accomplish this the information could be used to prevent human heart disease.

Early in the fall, brown or grizzly bears begin looking for a proper place to dig their dens, and may travel many miles before finding a suitable area. Generally, they seek a high, remote mountain slope where deep snow

Above: A polar bear on the move across the tundra. Unlike other bears, polar bears do not have a narrowly defined range, but rather they travel throughout the Arctic.

Above: Except for females with cubs, polar bears typically travel alone. However, groups have been observed to congregate around a particularly plentiful food source.

will lie until spring and serve as insulation. Here they often dig beneath the roots of a large tree to create their dens. Obstructing roots are chewed up, and loose rocks and earth are thrust through the narrow entrance by powerful forepaws. The bear will generally enter its den in October or November and stay in it for five or six months. During this time it will survive entirely on its accumulated fat, without any water other food. The males commonly emerge from the den in March or April, while females will sleep in until late April and May. When the brown bear comes out of its den, it will usually travel to lower elevations to reach vegetated areas. Its first food is often carrion from animals that did not survive the winter.

Mating season is from June through July, but embryos do not begin to develop until the mother begins her winter hibernation, often six months later. As with other bears, if the mother has not accumulated

Above: A grizzly (*lower right*) on the move, with Alaska's Mount McKinley visible in the distance. As seen here, rugged, treeless hillsides, heavy with dense brush, are typical grizzly habitat.

Above: The grizzly bear may weigh up to 1,000 pounds, and have
been recorded up to 1,500 pounds. Despite such mass, the bear's
powerful muscles allow it to be amazing agile.

enough fat to sustain herself, as well as developing cubs, the embryos may not develop. In January, usually one to three cubs, each weighing only a pound or less, are born while the mother sleeps after a gestation ranging from six to eight months. The cubs gain weight quickly from the mother's rich milk, which contains 33 percent fat. They often have reached 20 pounds by the time they come out of the den. As many as half of all cubs may not reach breeding age — a leading reason for the grizzly's low numbers. The young bears are usually weaned at five months of age, but may remain dependent upon their mother's milk for almost a year. They stay with their mother for two to three years.

While a juvenile brown or grizzly bear may reach breeding maturity at about four and a half to five and a half years of age, in some cases they may not breed until they are eight and a half. When they do reach breeding age, females breed at intervals of three or more years. However, males

Above: A pair of ten-day-old grizzly cubs and their mother.

Above: A ten-day-old grizzly cub nursing. Though still sightless and virtually helpless, this cub weighs 31 ounces, double her birth weight. The mother's milk contains 33 to 48 percent butterfat.

compete with each other for breeding opportunities and seek females every year. Brown and grizzly bears continue growing for 10 to 11 years, living from 15 to 30 years in the wild, or over 40 years in captivity. Grizzlies have been known to live and reproduce in Yellowstone Park at 25 years of age.

Since populations of grizzlies have been dwindling rapidly, many conservation plans have been put forward, but because the grizzly is not only an awe-inspiring, but a fearsome, beast, these plans are everywhere controversial and inadequately implemented.

Since the 1980s, the US Fish & Wildlife Service has undertaken a controversial plan to restore the grizzly bear in areas of the lower 48 states from which it had been absent for much of the twentieth century. The plan centered on placing grizzly populations in all of the ecosystems that are known to have suitable habitat. These six ecosystems were identified

Above and opposite: A grizzly bear cub at the age of three months, by which time the little bear will have learned to walk, and will have gained 20 pounds beyond his birth weight.

as the Yellowstone area (at the juncture of Idaho, Wyoming and Mon-tana), the Northern Continental Divide and Cabinet-Yaak area (north-western Montana), the Bitterroot (central Idaho and western Montana), the Selkirks (Idaho and eastern Washington), and the North Cascades (Washington).

The grizzly bear recovery effort met with some successes in the late 1980s and early 1990s. The grizzlies in the Yellowstone and the North Continental Divide ecosystems reached the recovery target by 1997. These results have been largely due to a cooperative effort among several organi-zations called The Interagency Grizzly Bear Committee. Established in 1983, the committee includes the US Forest Service; National Park Ser-vice; Bureau of Land Management; state agencies in Montana, Wyoming, Idaho, and Washington; Canadian wildlife management agencies; and Native American tribes, known in Canada as First Nations.

Above: A brown bear mother (known as a sow) takes her six-month-old cubs out to see a favorite fishing spot to begin to learn hunting skills.

Above: Even though these cubs are eating solid food, they still continue to nurse. Much of their diet consists of solid food by six or seven months, but nursing may last for a year or more.

As the US Fish & Wildlife Service embarked on an environmental impact statement process for grizzly bear restoration in the Bitterroot ecosystem of central Idaho and western Montana, several alternatives emerged. The plan most favored by US Fish & Wildlife was to place grizzly bears into a limited recovery area and designate them "experimental, nonessential," because many people in local communities felt livestock might be threatened. The goal of this plan was to increase the population number of grizzlies to 280 individuals in the next 50-100 years. Another approach, preferred by some conservation groups, was to retain protection for grizzlies under the Endangered Species Act.

In Canada, the British Columbia Grizzly Bear Conservation Strategy set forth by the Province of British Columbia's Ministry of Environment, Lands and Parks in 1995 also addressed the conservation of grizzly bear habitat. The ministry noted that the heart of the best remaining grizzly

Above: This mother brown bear has caught a salmon to share with her cubs. The young ones haven't begun to learn to fish, but by taking them to where salmon are caught, she is getting them used to the idea.

Above: Eating salmon is still a relatively new experience for these brown bear cubs, but soon this rich seafood will become a staple of their diet.

habitat in North America was in British Columbia. Its report suggested that unless steps were taken to conserve grizzly bear populations in British Columbia, the animal could disappear. The Grizzly Bear Conservation Strategy had four goals: 1) to maintain in perpetuity the diversity and abundance of grizzly bears and the ecosystems on which they depend throughout British Columbia, 2) to improve the management of grizzly bears and their interactions with humans, 3) to increase public knowledge of and involvement in grizzly bear management, and 4) to increase international cooperation in management and research of grizzly bears. The British Columbia Wildlife Federation, the oldest and the largest conservation organization in British Columbia, has been involved in numerous conservation projects throughout the province since 1959. Noting that it is concerned about the long-term viability of grizzly bear populations in British Columbia, the British Columbia Wildlife Federation has

Above: Two yearling grizzlies in mock battle. All bears play at fighting when they are young. Not only do they learn survival skills, but physical balance and coordination as well.

Above: This view of a pair of wrestling yearling grizzlies gives some
sense of their physical power and potential ferocity. When standing
on their hind legs, even yearlings may be seven to 10 feet tall.

said that it defines viability as a huntable population. This is because the group feels that a huntable population means a healthy population in the Kootenays and in the Okanagan, not just in the remote areas of the province. Despite concern over conservation, grizzly bear hunting continues, although it has been placed on the province's lottery system for the allocation of hunting opportunities, as it is in neighboring Alberta.

Even our Native Americans had widely varying attitudes towards this great bear, the world's largest terrestrial predator. John James Audubon wrote of the grizzly, "The Indians consider the slaughter of a grizzly bear a feat second only to scalping an enemy. Necklaces of the claws of this beast are worn as trophies among them. The audacity of these bears around Fort Union was remarkable."

However, grizzlies figured as creatures to be venerated in the origin myths of other Native Americans. According to one legend, the daughter

Above: This view of a grizzly sow and her two 18-month-old cubs shows the color variation possible among the species. Just as black bears may occasionally be brown, brown bears can be nearly black.

Above: The the color variation among grizzlies ranges from nearly black to the creamy, almost white, coat seen on this bear. The coloration seen here is more common in Montana and Wyoming than it is in Alaska.

of the Sky Spirit was taken from her home in California's Mount Shasta and left in the woods. She was found by a grizzly bear, who carried the little girl home. She was raised among the grizzly cubs, and she later wed the oldest son of the grizzlies. Their children were the first Native Americans, and consequently, the native people living around Mount Shasta would never kill a grizzly bear.

GETTING ALONG IN BEAR COUNTRY

Most people who see a bear in the wild consider it the highlight of their trip. The presence of these majestic creatures is a reminder of how privileged we are to share the continent's wilderness. However, bears are large, strong and don't like to feel threatened, so they are better observed at a distance.

Above: This grizzly bear appears as disheveled as he does grizzled. Among the names given to *Ursus arctos* by the native Blackfeet people of Montana and Alberta were "the hairy one" and "the unmentionable one."

Above: The grizzly has been known as "the yellow bear" or "the gray bear." Those bears with a noticeably silver-gray tinge to their coat are traditionally known as "silvertips."

Brown and grizzly bears have long been considered the most dangerous mammals in North America, and this may be true, although real danger of attack from this animal is often exaggerated. In general, all bears
attempt to avoid human contact and will not attack unless startled at close
quarters with young or when engrossed in a search for food. However, grizzlies are very unpredictable and impulsive in temperament, and are certainly far more aggressive than black bears. Serious incidents, although
usually not fatal, occur almost annually somewhere in the contiguous
United States, with most of these happening in and around Glacier
National Park, where grizzly populations are the highest.

Bears are curious, intelligent and potentially dangerous animals, but
undue fear of bears can be dangerous to both bears and people. Many bears
are killed each year by people who are afraid of them. People who respect
bears and know the proper behavior for bear territory understand what to

Above: A grizzly burying a caribou that
she has killed. She hopes to return for
another meal or two, or to share it with
her cubs. Burying the meat will keep it
away from eagles and other scavenging
birds.

Above: The grizzly pauses atop the caribou that she's buried. Grizzlies will hunt and kill members of the deer family, but they often simply eat animals killed by other causes.

do in a bear encounter so that neither they nor the bear will suffer from the experience. Most bears tend to avoid people. In most cases, given the opportunity, the bear will go his way and allow you to go yours.

Even in the national parks of the West, and in Alaska, surprisingly few people even see bears, though they are plentiful. In Alaska, where concentrations are the highest, only 20 people died in bear attacks between 1899 and 1985. Grizzly bear attacks in Montana's Glacier National Park, which have given the bear-attack folklore some of its most grisly tales, are also rare.

Such public agencies as the National Park Service; the US Fish & Wildlife Service; the US Forest Service; the US Bureau of Land Management; the Alaska Department of Fish & Game; the Alaska Department of Natural Resources, Divisions of Forestry and Parks and Outdoor Recreation; the Alaska Department of Public Safety, Division of Fish & Wildlife

Above: These brown bears have staked out Brooks Falls in Alaska's Katmai National Park to take advantage of the annual salmon run.

Above: A lone grizzly crossing a stream. The huge claws visible here are extremely effective in killing big game, but almost useless for climbing trees.

Protection; and the Alaska Natural History Association are universal in their recommendations regarding travel in bear country. They advise that if you are hiking through bear country, you should make your presence known, especially where the terrain or vegetation makes it hard to see. Bears will avoid you if they can, and they can if they know you're coming. Always let bears know you are there. Make noise, sing, talk loudly or tie a bell to your pack. If possible, travel with a group. Groups are noisier and easier for bears to detect. Avoid thick brush. If you can't, try to walk with the wind at your back so your scent will warn bears of your presence. Contrary to popular belief, bears can see almost as well as people, but they trust their noses much more than their eyes or ears.

Bears, like humans, use trails and roads. Don't set up camp close to a trail they might use. Detour around areas where you see or smell carcasses of fish or animals, or see scavengers congregated. A bear's food may be

Above and opposite: Brown bears wait patiently to snatch salmon swimming up Brooks Falls in Alaska.

there, and if the bear is nearby, it may defend the cache aggressively. Give bears plenty of room. Remember that bears are always looking for something to eat. They have only about six months to build up fat reserves for their long winter hibernation. Don't let them learn that human food or garbage is an easy meal. It is both foolish and illegal to feed bears, either on purpose or by leaving food or garbage that attracts them. Keep a clean camp and cook away from your tent. Store all food away from your campsite. Hang food out of reach of bears if possible. If no trees are available, store your food in airtight or specially designed bear-proof containers. Wash your dishes and avoid smelly food like bacon and smoked fish. Keep food smells off your clothing. Burn garbage completely in a hot fire and pack out the remains. Burying garbage is a waste of time. Bears have keen noses and are great diggers. If a bear approaches while you are fishing, stop fishing. If you have a fish on your line, don't let it splash. If that's not pos-

Above: A remarkable photograph of a brown bear catching a salmon in his mouth. Alaska runs are so rich with salmon that a clever bear can almost position himself in a particular place and simply open his mouth to get his dinner.

Above: A successful fisherman takes his catch to the gravel shore-
line to eat. The scavenging gulls will take the head and gills, which
the brown bears do not eat.

sible, cut your line. If a bear learns that it can obtain fish just by approach-
ing fishermen, it will return for more.

    If you encounter a bear, give it every opportunity to avoid you.
Attacks are rare and chances are, you are not in danger. A standing bear is
usually curious, not threatening. Most bears are interested only in protecting food, cubs or their territory. If they see you as not being a threat, they
will move on.

    Remember to let the bear know you are human. Talk to the bear in a
normal voice and help the bear recognize you. If a bear cannot tell what
you are, it may come closer or stand on its hind legs to get a better look or
smell. You may try to back away slowly and diagonally, but if the bear fol-
lows, don't run, because you can't outrun a bear. They have been clocked
at speeds up to 35 miles per hour, and like dogs, they will chase fleeing
animals. Bears often make bluff charges, sometimes to within 10 feet of

Above: When swimming upstream, the
salmon make powerful leaps to get to
the tops of falls. The brown bears take
advantage of their preoccupation with
their strenuous vaulting.

Above: A big brown bear pauses at the head of a waterfall, ready to fish. He must be extremely careful with his footing on the slippery rocks and in the fast-moving water.

their adversary, without making contact. Continue waving your arms and talking to the bear. If the bear gets too close, raise your voice, bang pots and pans or use noisemakers. However, never imitate bear sounds or make a high-pitched squeal.

If a brown bear actually touches you, fall to the ground and play dead. Lie flat on your stomach, or curl up in a ball with your hands behind your neck. Typically a brown bear will break off its attack when it feels the threat has been eliminated. Remain motionless for as long as possible. If you move, a brown bear may return and renew its attack and you must again play dead. If you are attacked by a black bear, fight back vigorously.

In most cases, bears are not a threat, but they do deserve our respect and attention. When traveling in bear country, keep alert and enjoy the opportunity to see these great animals in their natural environment.

Above: The bear waits patiently as the salmon attempts to fling itself to the top of the falls.

Above: Patience pays off for the brown bear. During the Alaska salmon runs of June and July, each brown bear may consume 60 to 100 fish each day.

Above: A brown bear enjoys her salmon at the top of the falls. These
bears can eat 35 pounds of fish each day, but during a salmon run,
their daily intake may reach 90 pounds.

Above: The brown bears may use their claws as well as their jaws to catch fish, but they rarely use their paws to slap a fish out of the water.

Above: The spectacle of brown bears fishing Brooks Falls in Katmai National Park is enjoyed not only by people, but by other bears. This attentive group, which appears as though they are attending a seminar, may actually be young bears who are studying the fine points of technique from an experienced hand.

Opposite: These bears seem almost transfixed by the sight of rushing water and the salmon leaping against the flow. Brown bears also fish for other species, but the salmon run is the largest concentration of fish on which they feed.

INDEX